Ideas, Inventions, and Innovators

THE GREATEST
BUILDINGS
AND STRUCTURES

BY GRACE JONES

CRABTREE
PUBLISHING COMPANY
WWW.CRABTREEBOOKS.COM

CRABTREE
PUBLISHING COMPANY
WWW.CRABTREEBOOKS.COM

Published in Canada
Crabtree Publishing
616 Welland Avenue
St. Catharines, ON
L2M 5V6

Published in the United States
Crabtree Publishing
PMB 59051
350 Fifth Ave, 59th Floor
New York, NY 10118

Published in 2019 by Crabtree Publishing Company

Author: Grace Jones

Editorial director: Kathy Middleton

Editors: Madeline Tyler, Petrice Custance

Proofreader: Melissa Boyce

Designer: Gareth Liddington

Prepress technician: Tammy McGarr, Ken Wright

Print coordinator: Katherine Berti

Images

Shutterstock: 135pixels p 5 (3rd row, left); shootmybusiness p 6 (bottom); aphotostory p 11 (bottom); Zoran Karapancev p 13 (bottom); Jane Rix p 15 (bottom left); Takashi Images p 17 (bottom); Albo p 19 (top); Alessandro Colle p 19 (bottom right); credit: S-F p 28; slava296 p 29 (top); Bulatovych p 29 (bottom)

Wikimedia: title page; pp 6 (top right), 16, 22 (top); p 7 (bottom); p 10; p 11; p 12 (top); p 12; p 13 (top, middle); p 14 (top); p 15 (top, middle); p 17 (top, middle); p 18; p 19 (bottom left); p 20 (top); p 21–26; 27 (bottom)

All other images from Shutterstock

All facts, statistics, web addresses and URLs in this book were verified as valid and accurate at time of writing. No responsibility for any changes to external websites or references can be accepted by either the author or publisher.

Printed in the U.S.A./122018/CG20181005

Library and Archives Canada Cataloguing in Publication

Jones, Grace, 1990-, author
    The greatest buildings and structures / Grace Jones.

(Ideas, inventions, and innovators)
Includes index.
Issued in print and electronic formats.
ISBN 978-0-7787-5826-6 (hardcover).--
ISBN 978-0-7787-5970-6 (softcover).--
ISBN 978-1-4271-2237-7 (HTML)

    1. Architecture--Juvenile literature. 2. Buildings--Juvenile literature. I. Title.

NA2555.J66 2018   j720   C2018-905460-3
                                      C2018-905461-1

Library of Congress Cataloging-in-Publication Data

Names: Jones, Grace, 1990- author.
Title: The greatest buildings and structures / Grace Jones.
Description: New York : Crabtree Publishing Company, 2019. |
  Series: [Ideas, inventions, and innovators] | Includes index.
Identifiers: LCCN 2018043641 (print) | LCCN 2018045070 (ebook) |
  ISBN 9781427122377 (Electronic) |
  ISBN 9780778758266 (hardcover) |
  ISBN 9780778759706 (pbk.)
Subjects: LCSH: Architecture--Miscellanea--Juvenile literature. |
  Historic buildings--Miscellanea--Juvenile literature.
Classification: LCC NA200 (ebook) | LCC NA200 .J63 2019 (print) |
  DDC 720--dc23
LC record available at https://lccn.loc.gov/2018043641

CONTENTS

THE GREATEST BUILDINGS AND STRUCTURES

• •

Buildings and structures are the places where we live, sleep, eat, learn, work, and worship. However, many buildings and structures are more than just a place to rest our heads, or something to be admired from a distance. Buildings and structures are a symbol of what human beings can achieve. They can also tell us a thousand stories. Through their design and **engineering**, buildings and structures can tell us much about the history and the culture of a place and its people.

Skyscraper

House

Mosque

What is Stonehenge and what does it tell us about prehistoric Britain?

How were the ancient Egyptian pyramids built?

How long did it take to build the Great Wall of China?

What did the ancient Romans use the Colosseum for?

Why was the Tower of London built?

Why did King Louis XIV build the Palace of Versailles?

Why is it taking so long to finish building La Sagrada Família?

Is the Eiffel Tower the most famous structure in the world?

How tall is the Empire State Building?

Is the Golden Gate Bridge the most iconic bridge in the world?

How long did it take to build the Sydney Opera House?

How many world records does the Burj Khalifa hold?

Let's go on a journey to find the answers to these questions and more...

STONEHENGE

· ·

Stonehenge is a collection of large stones that were **erected** in several stages over 5,000 years ago in Wiltshire, England. Historians are still not sure why Stonehenge was built, but some experts believe Stonehenge could have been used for religious **ceremonies**, as a burial ground, or for **rituals** to mark the changing of the seasons.

Stonehenge is made from two types of stones. The smaller stones, known as bluestones, are a variety of stones not found in the area around Stonehenge. The larger stones, made from local sandstone, are called sarsens. The largest of the sarsen stones are 30 feet (9 m) tall and weigh 25 tons (22.6 metric tons). It has been determined that the builders of Stonehenge transported the bluestones over 236 miles (380 km) from Wales.

The builders only had tools made from wood, stone, and rope, so no one is entirely sure how they managed to transport the stones and build such a huge structure!

Stonehenge is made of two circles—an inner circle built from bluestones, and an outer circle built from sarsens.

In 2013, **archaeologists** found buried at Stonehenge more than 50,000 human bones belonging to 63 different people. Some of these bones are up to 5,000 years old. This has led many experts to believe Stonehenge may have been built as a burial ground for ancient people. The stones may be very early gravestones that mark the graves of members of the same family, community, or religious group.

Others believe the position of the stones is linked to the position of the Sun during the summer **solstice**, or the longest day of the year, and the winter solstice, or the shortest day of the year. People may have gathered at Stonehenge on these days for ceremonies.

The entrance to the circle faces the rising Sun on the summer solstice.

Stonehenge on the summer solstice

GREAT PYRAMID

Thousands of years ago, the ancient Egyptians built huge structures called pyramids. These pyramids were burial sites for **pharaohs**. The Great Pyramid, the oldest and largest of the three pyramids of Giza, consists of 2.3 million stone blocks. Each block weighs about 2.5 tons (2.3 metric tons). How were the ancient Egyptians able to build such an amazing structure? It seems an impossible task without modern building equipment, such as cranes. Somehow, the ancient Egyptians managed one of the greatest building achievements in history.

No one knows exactly how long it took to build the pyramid, but most estimates range from 10 to 30 years during the pharaoh Khufu's reign, which began in around 2551 B.C.E. Some experts believe it took between 15,000 and 40,000 people to build the huge pyramid.

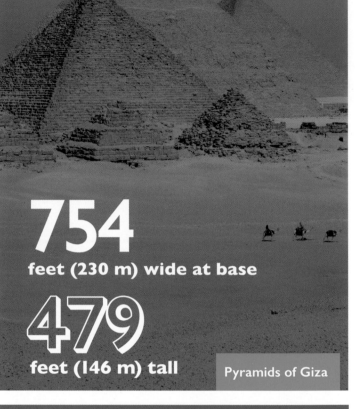

754
feet (230 m) wide at base

479
feet (146 m) tall

Pyramids of Giza

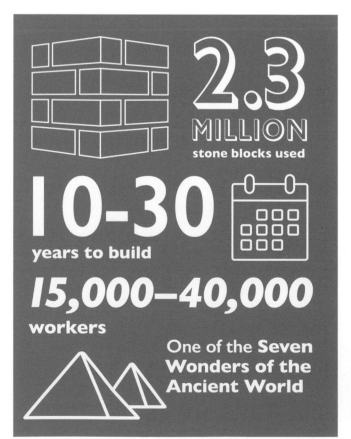

2.3 MILLION
stone blocks used

10-30
years to build

15,000–40,000
workers

One of the **Seven Wonders of the Ancient World**

The Great Sphinx of Giza was built around the same time as the Great Pyramid.

The Egyptians had to transport the heavy stones from faraway locations to Giza. Each block of stone had to be cut and hammered into shape near the **quarries** from where they were taken. The blocks are thought to have been moved on land using large sleds or ramps that could be pushed or pulled by groups of workers, and then transported by boat along the Nile River.

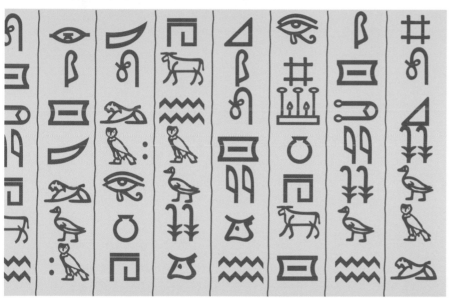

Many ancient Egyptian pyramids have survived until the present day. It is partly because of these amazing structures that we know so much about the language and culture of the ancient Egyptians. The pyramids have also inspired **architects** around the world. The Pyramide du Louvre in Paris, France, is a glass structure inspired by the ancient Egyptian pyramids.

The granite stones that make up the pharaoh's main chamber inside the pyramid were transported by boat along the Nile River from the city of Aswan—over 500 miles (800 km) away!

GREAT WALL OF CHINA

The Great Wall of China stretches across the country's northern border. It is believed to have once been up to 13,000 miles (21,000 km) long. Parts of the wall are no longer standing, but it is still the longest human-made structure in the world.

2,000
Parts of the wall are more than 2,000 years old.

10 MILLION
visitors every year

It is made from brick, stone, sand, and soil.

46
The tallest part of the wall is nearly 46 feet (14 m) tall.

32
At its widest point, the wall is 32 feet (10 m) wide.

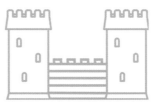

The wall was very well defended with towers and soldiers to protect the people of China from invading armies.

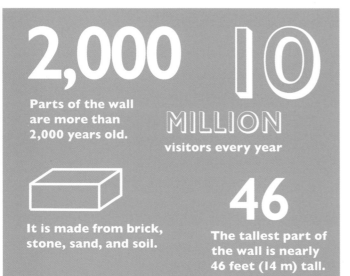

MONGOLIA

MANCHURIA

INNER MONGOLIA

...an Pass

• Shanhai Pass

Beijing

Bo Hai Sea

CHINA

...etan Plateau

The construction of the Great Wall began over 2,000 years ago. At first, the wall was made up of many smaller, separate walls. Years later, all of these walls were joined together. The Great Wall was designed to be three times the height of an average person.

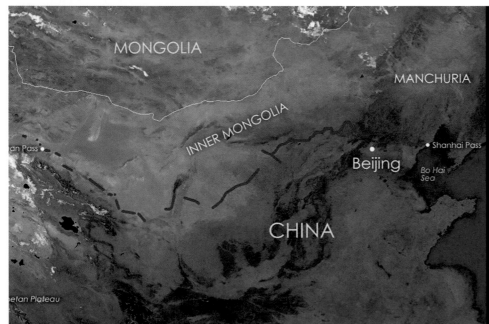

Because of its size, many workers would have been needed to build the wall. Historians believe that hundreds of thousands of soldiers, **peasants**, and prisoners were forced to build the wall. It is thought that many people died during its construction because of the dangerous working conditions. Heavy building materials were often carried by workers on their backs as they climbed up the steep mountainsides.

Parts of the Great Wall are built in deserts and near mountains, which would have made construction very difficult for the builders.

The Great Wall was built, rebuilt, made longer, and repaired in many different stages over 2,000 years. Nearly one third of the original wall has disappeared due to **erosion** and human damage.

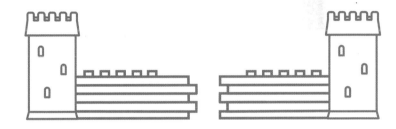

The Great Wall of China displays the impressive building skills of ancient Chinese **civilizations**. It is also one of the largest ancient structures in the world. It tells us a lot about ancient Chinese culture and continues to be one of the most popular tourist destinations in the world.

The Great Wall is wide enough in some places for a car to be driven on it!

COLOSSEUM

The Colosseum is a large amphitheater built by the ancient Romans in the city of Rome, Italy between 72 and 80 C.E. An amphitheater is an open, circular building with a main area in the middle used for sports or **dramatic** events. The main area of an amphitheater is surrounded by seating so people can watch the events.

620
feet (189 m) long

↑187
feet (57 m)
tall

In ancient Rome, the Colosseum was called the *Amphitheatrum Flavium*.

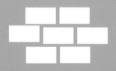
Between 50,000 and 80,000 people could watch the events held at the Colosseum.

The Colosseum was the largest amphitheater built by the Romans.

Emperor Vespasian began construction of the Colosseum in around 72 C.E., and Emperor Titus finished it in 80 C.E. It is made of a mixture of stone and concrete, and has three floors. The Colosseum was built by teams of skilled **stonemasons**, artists, and **engineers**, as well as an estimated 100,000 prisoners and **enslaved** people who transported the heavy stones.

The invention of concrete sped up the building of the Colosseum. Some historians believe that if there was no concrete, the Colosseum could not have been built.

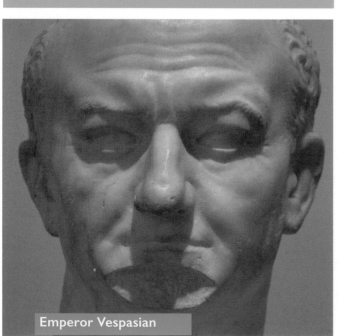
Emperor Vespasian

Emperor Titus

The Colosseum in Rome was used mostly for events involving **gladiators**. Gladiators would fight against each other until only one remained alive. Sometimes they would fight against wild animals, such as lions or even bears. The Colosseum was also used for plays, the **execution** of prisoners, and sometimes it was filled with water to hold sea battles.

The Colosseum is one of the most iconic buildings of ancient Rome. It was built using the latest arts, engineering, and building methods of the time. Today, parts of the Colosseum are missing but it is still considered a **symbol** of the Roman Empire. It is also one of the most popular tourist attractions in the world.

Today, the floor inside the Colosseum is missing. Only the passageways underground can be seen.

 Many of the events held at the Colosseum were free for ancient Romans to enjoy.

The influence of the techniques and designs used during the building of the Colosseum can be seen in many famous stadiums that exist today.

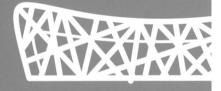

Beijing National Stadium (also called the Bird's Nest), China

The Colosseum, Italy

TOWER OF LONDON

The Tower of London is a castle in London, England. Construction began in 1078 and took about 20 years to complete. Over the last 900 years, many parts of the Tower have been added and restored. Throughout history it has been used for many different things, including a prison, **barracks**, and a house for the royal family.

William the Conqueror from France successfully invaded England in 1066. After this, he was afraid the people of England might harm him. He ordered the building of many castles to protect him from **rebellion**. One of these was the White Tower, which was the first part of the Tower of London to be built.

White Tower

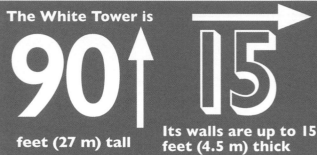

The White Tower is

90 feet (27 m) tall

15 Its walls are up to 15 feet (4.5 m) thick

Tower of London

ENTRY TO THE TRAITORS' GATE

For hundreds of years, the Tower of London was used to hold important prisoners. If they were found guilty, they would be taken to be hanged or executed in front of large crowds. Some of the most famous prisoners held in the Tower of London include Queen Elizabeth I and two of Henry VIII's wives, Anne Boleyn and Catherine Howard, who were both executed.

Anne Boleyn

Catherine Howard

The Tower of London has also been nicknamed the "Bloody Tower" because of the gruesome end many of its prisoners met.

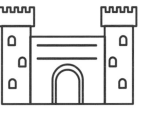

Elizabeth I

Elizabeth I was put in the tower by her sister Mary, but was never executed.

Today, the Tower of London is open to the public as a museum. It is also home to the **Crown Jewels.** As well as being an amazing **feat** of construction, it is a place that tells many stories of England's interesting—and often gruesome—history.

The Beefeaters are guards at the Tower of London. They are mainly responsible for looking after the Crown Jewels. The Beefeaters are very popular with tourists!

PALACE OF VERSAILLES

The Palace of Versailles (pronounced Ver-sigh) is one of the greatest achievements in French architecture. It is a royal palace located around 12 miles (20 km) outside of Paris. The Palace was originally a royal hunting lodge and later a small castle, but King Louis XIV transformed it into a grand palace during his reign.

The Palace now contains over 2,300 rooms.

King Louis XIV began construction of his grand palace in 1661. He built the Palace because he wanted to move his **court** and **government** from Paris to Versailles. He believed that by doing so he would have more control over the government and his **nobles**.

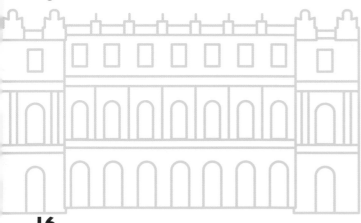

King Louis XIV moved the French court and government to Versailles in 1682.

Between 1661 and 1710, the castle was transformed into one of the grandest palaces in the world. Every part of the Palace was designed to celebrate the King. Famous architects, landscape artists, and painters worked to create Louis XIV's vision of the Palace and its gardens. One of the most famous rooms, the Hall of Mirrors, is over 230 feet (70 m) long. It contains many mirrors, glass chandeliers, and a painted ceiling.

The Palace of Versailles is one of the greatest achievements in the history of France. The building of the Palace allowed Louis XIV to lead France and better control his government and his court. The Palace is now a national museum, and tourists continue to be amazed by its breathtaking architecture, rooms, and gardens.

The Palace of Versailles is one of the world's largest palaces. It covers an area of over 2,000 acres (809 ha).

The kings that ruled after Louis XIV continued adding to and improving the Palace right up until the **French Revolution** in 1789.

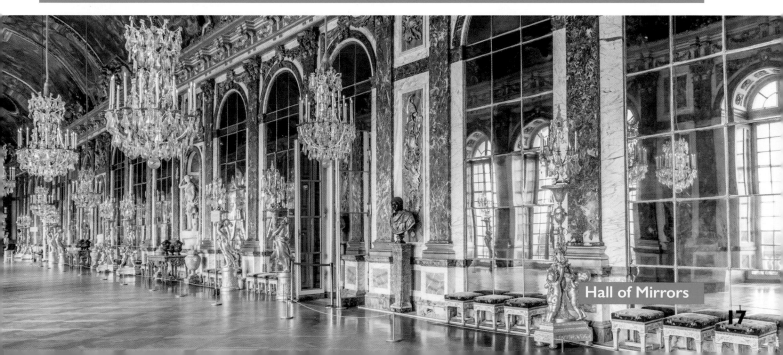

Hall of Mirrors

LA SAGRADA FAMÍLIA

La Sagrada Família is a large **Roman Catholic** church located in Barcelona, Spain. It is one of the most famous and unique churches in the world—partly because it is still being built!

1882
The construction of the church began in 1882. It is still being worked on today.

558
When complete, the highest point of the church will be 558 feet (170 meters) tall.

The architect, Antoni Gaudí, is buried in the church.

18
When it is finished, the church will have 18 towers.

In the beginning, builders followed Gaudí's sketches and plaster models. Today, they follow plans designed on computers.

Antoni Gaudí

In the 1800s, a religious group planned to build a church in Barcelona in honor of the **Holy Family**, or *Sagrada Família* in Spanish. The architect, Francisco de Paula del Villar, began to work on the church. However, Villar and the group disagreed over the design. In 1883, Antoni Gaudí took over the construction. He worked on the church for more than 33 years, until his death in 1926. When Gaudí died, the church was only 25 percent complete.

Many people refer to La Sagrada Família as a **cathedral**, but it is actually a church.

Work on the church has taken so long because Gaudí's design is very complicated. He wanted to represent nature in the architecture. There are no straight lines or sharp angles in the building, only curves, which represent the lines found in nature.

The pillars inside the church were designed to look like trees.

From the beginning, the cost of building La Sagrada Família has been paid through donations.

More than three million people visit La Sagrada Família every year to admire its impressive architecture. The entrance fees help cover the building costs, which are estimated to be $28 million per year. Construction of the church is planned to be completed in 2026 to **commemorate** the 100th anniversary of Gaudí's death.

EIFFEL TOWER

The Eiffel Tower in Paris, France is 1,063 feet (324 m) tall. An engineer named Gustave Eiffel designed and built the Tower between 1887 and 1889. It took just two years, two months, and five days to complete the huge structure that is now considered a symbol of France.

The Eiffel Tower was originally designed for the 1889 **World's Fair** to celebrate the 100th anniversary of the French Revolution. It was only supposed to be there for 20 years, but it was saved and used for experiments involving communication and radio. Since then, it has been regularly improved and changed to become the most popular tourist attraction in France.

The French Revolution began in 1789. The royal family was overthrown by the French people who set up a new government, called a **republic**.

7
More than seven million people visit every year

Named after Gustave Eiffel, the engineer who designed it

1,063 feet (324 m) tall

41 The world's tallest human–made structure for 41 years

Some 18,000 pieces that were used to make parts of the Tower were designed, cut and put together into larger pieces in Gustave Eiffel's factory. Between 150 and 300 workers put smaller parts together to make larger ones in the factory, but some had to be assembled at the site. To erect the Tower, wooden **scaffolding** and small cranes were used.

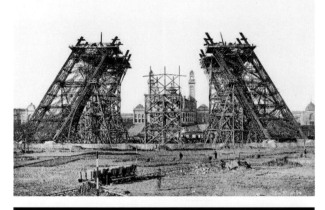

Over 8,000 tons (7,250 metric tons) of iron and 66 tons (60 metric tons) of paint were used to construct the Eiffel Tower.

The Eiffel Tower has become one of most iconic and visited structures in the world. Gustave Eiffel is also recognized for achieving amazing feats of architecture and engineering. His building method of putting together parts before erecting structures inspired the construction of many other buildings and structures, such as the Statue of Liberty in New York.

EMPIRE STATE BUILDING

The Empire State Building is located on Fifth Avenue in New York City. From 1931 to 1970 it was the world's tallest building. Now the world's 28th-tallest building, it receives more than 3.5 million visitors every year.

102
floors

1,250
feet (381 m) tall

1931
The building opened its doors in 1931.

80
On a clear day, visitors can see more than 80 miles (129 km) from the 102nd-floor observation deck.

It got its name from the nickname for New York, which is often called the "Empire State."

A team of architects—Richard Harold Shreve, William F. Lamb, and Arthur Loomis Harmon—designed the Empire State Building in the art deco style, which was very popular at the time. Art deco is a style of architecture and decoration that focuses on elegance and glamor, and symbolizes wealth and sophistication. The Empire State Building is one of the most famous examples of art deco architecture. It is also an inspirational structure that, for many, symbolizes American success, wealth, and power.

Construction of the Empire State Building began in 1930 and took just over a year to complete. Around 3,400 workers were involved in the construction of the building. They erected the building very quickly and, on average, four-and-a-half floors were built every week.

The Empire State Building Run-Up is a race that has been held every year since 1978. Runners from around the world race each other up 1,576 steps to the building's 86th floor. The record time, 9 minutes and 33 seconds, was set in 2003 by Australian Paul Crake.

GOLDEN GATE BRIDGE

The Golden Gate Bridge is a **suspension** bridge that links San Francisco to Marin County, in California. It is one of the most famous bridges in the world due to its recognizable and unique design. Until 1964, the Golden Gate Bridge was the longest suspension bridge in the world. It weighs 887,000 tons (804,673 metric tons).

The Golden Gate Bridge was designed by Joseph Strauss, Irving Morrow, and Leon Moisseiff. Construction began in January 1933. Since opening in 1937, more than two billion cars have crossed the bridge. About 110,000 cars cross it every day. The one-billionth driver, a dentist named Dr. Arthur Molinari, crossed the bridge on February 22, 1985. He received a construction hat and champagne as congratulations.

1.7
miles (2.7 km) long

746
feet (227 m) high

90
feet (27 m) wide

1.2
million steel **rivets** were used in its construction

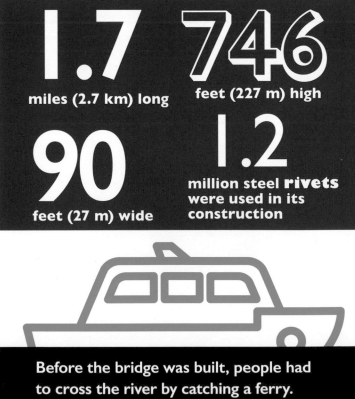

Before the bridge was built, people had to cross the river by catching a ferry. The ferry trip took about 20 minutes.

Builders and engineers started with the two towers at either end of the bridge: one was built on land and the other was built over 980 feet (300 m) out into the water. Rough waters, strong winds, and thick fog made the building of the bridge very difficult, but they finally finished it four years later, in 1937. Since its opening, the bridge has been closed due to bad weather only three times.

$35 million

was the cost to build the bridge. It was completed on time and within budget.

83,000

tons (75,000 metric tons) of steel were used in the making of the bridge.

The Golden Gate Bridge is one of the most famous landmarks in America. The unique structure is not just recognized for its beauty and architecture, but as one of the world's greatest building accomplishments. Many people believe that the Golden Gate Bridge is now the most photographed bridge in the world.

SYDNEY OPERA HOUSE

The Sydney Opera House is an arts center located on Sydney Harbour in Sydney, Australia. It includes seven performance venues that host about 1,500 different performances every year. The building is famous and instantly recognizable due to its unique and modern style of architecture.

 The largest venue, the Concert Hall, seats 2,679 people. The smallest venue, the Utzon room, seats 210 people.

394
feet (120 m) wide

600
feet (183 m) long

In 1956, the Australian government decided to build the Sydney Opera House. A competition was held, and 233 designs were entered by architects from around the world. In 1957, Danish architect Jørn Utzon was announced the winner. Jørn Utzon's design became the Sydney Opera House standing today.

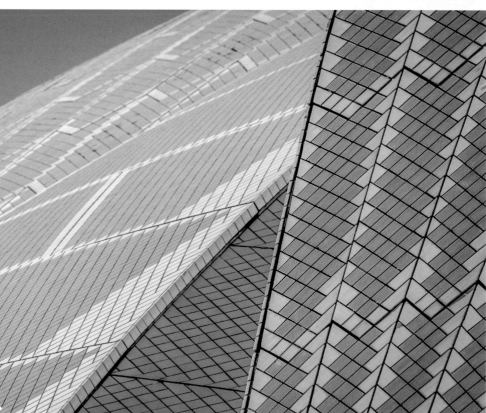

In 1959, construction of the building began with a workforce of over 10,000 people. The "sails" at the top of the building were each built using three huge tower cranes that were specially made in France. The roof is covered with more than one million tiles. Originally planned to take four years to build, the construction ended up taking 14 years. Queen Elizabeth opened the building on October 20, 1973.

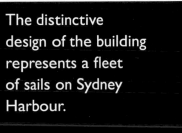

The distinctive design of the building represents a fleet of sails on Sydney Harbour.

The Sydney Opera House is Australia's top tourist attraction, with more than eight million visitors every year. The building is recognized as being **eco-friendly**. Its heating and cooling system is powered by seawater taken from the harbor.

BURJ KHALIFA

The Burj Khalifa is currently the world's tallest building. Located in Dubai, United Arab Emirates, construction began on the skyscraper in 2004. It opened to the public in 2010. Construction on the Burj Khalifa cost an estimated $1.5 billion. Now Dubai's most popular attraction, nearly two million people visit the building every year.

As well as being the tallest building in the world, the Burj Khalifa holds six other world records:

- tallest free-standing structure
- highest number of stories
- highest outdoor observation deck
- tallest elevator
- highest restaurant
- highest New Year's Eve display of fireworks

2,717
feet (828 meters) tall

163 floors

The main elevators climb 1,654 feet (504 meters)

2,909
number of steps to top

At the height of building, there were 12,000 people working on the Burj Khalifa every day. It took 22 million hours to complete. The building is made of 110,000 tons (99,790 metric tons) of **reinforced** concrete and 55,000 tons (49,895 metric tons) of reinforced steel.

The building's 24,348 windows are made of **reflective** glass panels with an anti-glare shield. This protects the building from the extreme desert sun and temperatures, as well as strong winds. It takes 36 workers between three and four months to clean all the windows!

The building's elevators are some of the fastest in the world. They travel at 33 feet (10 meters) per second.

In 2020, the Burj Khalifa will lose the title of tallest building in the world to Jeddah Tower, in Jeddah, Saudi Arabia. Planned to be 3,281 feet (1 km) tall, construction began on Jeddah Tower in 2013.

GLOSSARY

ancient The very distant past

archaeologists Historians who study buried ruins and ancient objects in order to learn about human history

architects People who design buildings

barracks A building or buildings where soldiers live

cathedral A church that is a seat of a bishop

ceremonies Formal occasions celebrating achievements, people, or events

civilizations The societies, cultures, and ways of life of certain areas

commemorate To celebrate or show respect for an event or a person

court The people who formally assist a king or queen

Crown Jewels A collection of precious jewelry, metalwork, and clothes worn by the kings and queens of England

dramatic Relating to drama or acting

eco-friendly Not harmful to the environment

engineering The process of designing and building engines and machinery

enslaved Stripped of one's freedom and forced to do work for someone else

erected Built in an upright position

erosion The gradual wearing away of something by water, wind, or other natural agent

execution The act of putting someone to death

feat A thing that is difficult to achieve

French Revolution The uprising of French citizens against the monarchy, lasting from 1789 to 1799

gladiators Trained fighters in ancient Rome

government The group of people with the authority to run a country and decide its laws

Holy Family In Christianity, the family consisting of Jesus, Mary, and Joseph

iconic Widely recognized or famous

nobles People of high rank

peasants Poor workers who belonged to the lowest social class

pharaohs Kings or queens of ancient Egypt

prehistoric Any period of history that occurred before the presence of writing

quarries Large, human-made holes in the ground from which natural building materials, such as stone and sand, are dug

rebellion When people fight against their government, leader, or ruler

reflective To prevent the passage of something, such as light, and cause it to change direction

reinforced Made stronger with additional materials

republic A nation where the government is elected by the people

LEARNING MORE

rituals A series of ordered actions that take place during religious ceremonies

rivets Pins or bolts used in building to hold two pieces of material together

Roman Catholic A branch of Christianity

scaffolding A temporary structure that keeps something in place

Seven Wonders of the Ancient World The seven ancient structures of the world that are considered to be the most important

solstice Twice a year when the Sun reaches its highest or lowest point in the sky

stonemasons People who cut and build with stone

suspension Hung or attached to something from above rather than being supported from below

symbol Something that represents something else

World's Fair An international exhibition of scientific, industrial, and artistic achievements

BOOKS

Ancient Worlds Inside Out (Series). Crabtree Publishing, 2017.

Brasch, Nicolas. *Amazing Built Structures (The Technology Behind)*. Smart Apple Media, 2011.

Solway, Andrew. *Civil Engineering and the Science of Structures*. Crabtree Publishing, 2013.

WEBSITES

Visit this site for tons of information about amazing buildings and structures around the world:
www.factmonster.com/cool-stuff/ buildings-and-structures

Check out this site for more information on famous structures:
www.kids-world-travel-guide.com/ top-10-famous-landmarks.html

Learn more about the coolest skyscrapers in the world here:
https://kids.nationalgeographic. com/explore/awesome-8-hub/ skyscrapers/

INDEX